ENDFINITY

_hydrus

Published by: Hydrus

Photography & Illustrated Art by: Hydrus

Cover Design by: Cleo Moran - Devoted Pages Designs

Formatting by: Cleo Moran - Devoted Pages Designs

https://www.devotedpages.com

Proofreading: Amina Jojo Dahmouche

Manufactured in the United States of America

The Library of Congress Cataloging-in-Publication Data is available upon request.

Paperback ISBN: 979-8-9856109-9-4

E-Book ISBN: 979-8-9856109-8-7

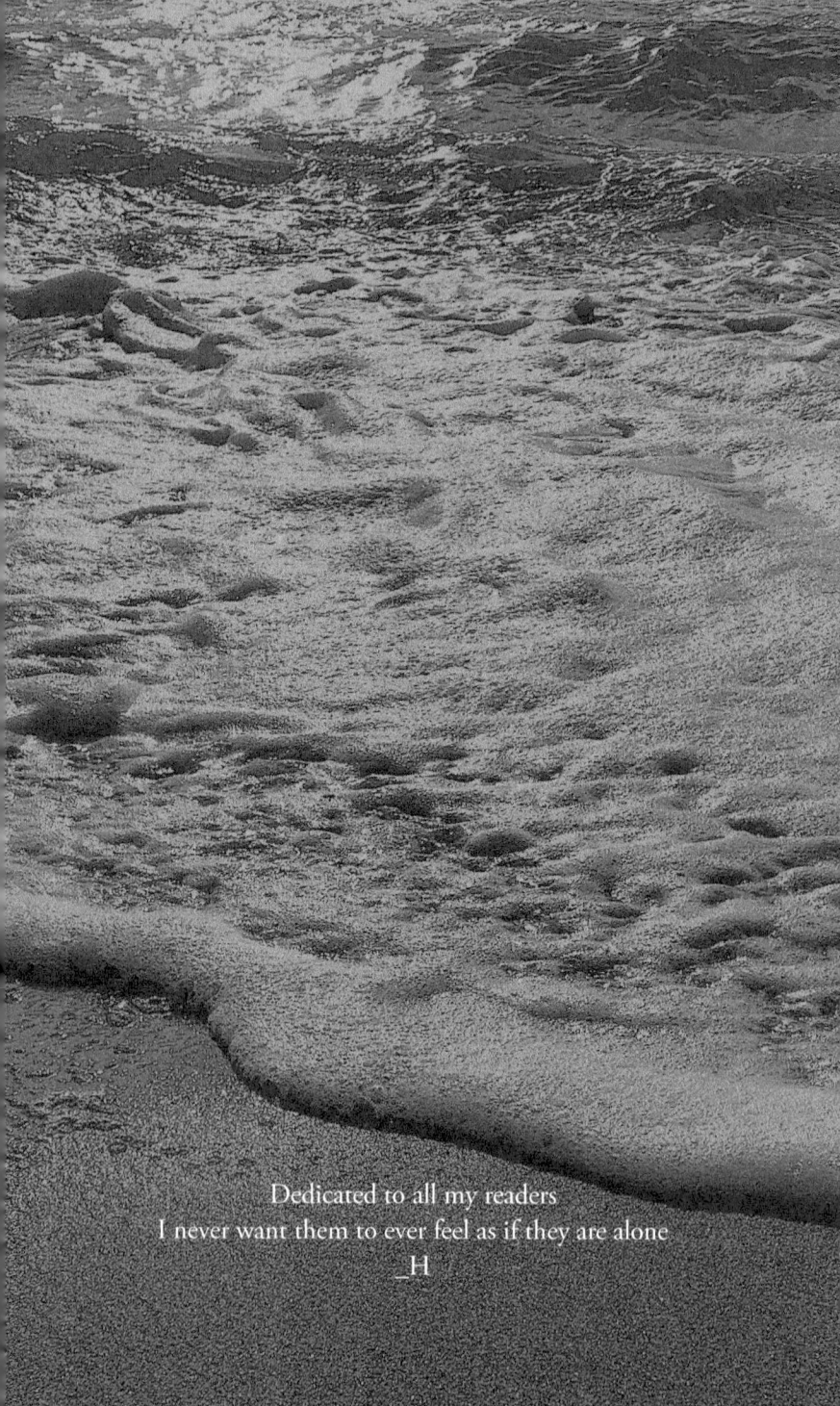

Dedicated to all my readers
I never want them to ever feel as if they are alone
_H

ENDfinity

Everyone deserves love, understanding, to be heard,
and, above all, hope.

As I began to write this book, penning thoughts and ideas about
this very notion, I found myself in a place where the world
sometimes appears overwhelmingly dark. I believe our minds and
hearts resonate with that darkness too. Surrounded by negativity,
often stemming from those around us, we may begin to doubt
ourselves and our convictions.

I hope that by reading this book, you can find some direction,
motivation, or perhaps even inspiration. A glimmer of light
during dark and challenging times. I hope you will recognize that
we all possess our own beauty. That each and every one of us has
the power to shape our own destinies, rewrite our own stories,
and uncover the true beauty that resides within us all. There is so
much to explore, see, and experience out there. Our own
horizons are limitless and vast.

We all deserve to venture and pursue our own happiness, and it
begins with the infinite ways we need to believe in and love
ourselves.

Trust in the beauty that I see in you

_hydrus

Voices that taunt
Even from birth
Are not owed time
To question your worth

It's all only noise
Meant to disrupt
You cannot just concede
They must not corrupt

Be strong and believe
For all that you are
Heavens will weave
As they erase every scar

Be true to your person
And your beauty within
Stop blaming yourself
For everyone's sins

Liberated
_hydrus

Be the fearless queen
That can't be tamed
Build your empire
Upon his pain

Let them know
Who truly rules
Impale the chest
Of the foolish fool

Vicious
_hydrus

Her wings left me breathless
And her dreams were my escape

_hydrus

ENDfinity

My little Angel
Far from home
In my heart
Is where you roam

Watchful eyes
From up above
Bless your steps
With all their love

Pillar
_hydrus

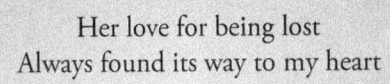

Her love for being lost
Always found its way to my heart

_hydrus

The world awaits
It's in your grasp
Don't hesitate
Just make your path

Your will is strong
Focus is clear
Believe in you
Undo all fears

Faith
_hydrus

Quiet the noise
Make it fade away
It feeds off your happiness
It just wants to stay

Deafening tones
Made to confuse
Take control of your life
You have nothing to lose

Choir
_hydrus

ENDfinity

Eternity will never be enough for us
Forever is

_hydrus

Feed us your garden
And live off the earth
Between all the petals
Our love finds its thirst

May the heavens now rain
Flooding these fields
Drenching your seasons
And the bliss it will yield

Bounty
_hydrus

Find strength in your ability
To challenge your own expectations

_hydrus

Wash your tears
In my hands
Feeling your pain
I understand

They left too soon
Then darkness came
Life is just cruel
You are not to blame

Wavering
_hydrus

I want to find myself in you
and lose myself in your soul

_hydrus

You are the armor
I never had
You became my shield
When all was bad

Your words the spears
Enemies the prey
I thank the heavens
For you each day

Guardian
_hydrus

Judging words
And haunting eyes
Taunt your look
As a disguise

Be yourself
Fuck their words
You are in charge
They are absurd

They cannot feel
The pain inside
Every ordeal
The ones you hide

Only you
Can bear the truth
Keep it inside
Its own recluse

And when you choose
To share your heart
You can decide
Pick what departs

You are in control
Of every smile
And the joy they stole
As they chose denial

Haven
_hydrus

Even in darkness, your beauty
Needs no explanation, definition or excuses...
It just simply unapologetically exists

_hydrus

ENDfinity

Don't fight the universe
Let its stars paint your night

Have it eat your early mornings
As you drink its thirsty light

Calling
_hydrus

I know our perfect ending
Because of our beautiful beginning

_hydrus

Sleep doesn't come
Its absence is here
When darkness arrives
It wakes every fear

Sunlight feels distant
Yet it awaits every day
Believe in tomorrow
Leave the demons at bay

Unwavering
_hydrus

Work hard
For every dream awaits
Your divine sacrifice

_hydrus

Let me be the sponge
That absorbs the rain
Wipes all the tears
Heals all your pain

Soaks any doubts
The heart replays
By your side
I will always stay

Evermore
_hydrus

She is my never ending trance
A blurry daze with bliss
An unrelenting dream
So precious with every kiss

Limitless
_hydrus

ENDfinity

You are so undefinable
Yet you are beautiful beyond meaning

_hydrus

Stretch those wings
Escape your cage
It's what you bleed
That makes me crave

Feed the hunger
That beats inside
Free those flames
Burn the world alive

Ignite
_hydrus

Challenges are simply
Another chance to prove them wrong

_hydrus

You are my perfect everything
Infinitely beautiful and intoxicatingly you

_hydrus

Every moment
I am not with you
Life feels empty
In all I do

A flightless bird
Without its wings
I need you back
So my soul can sing

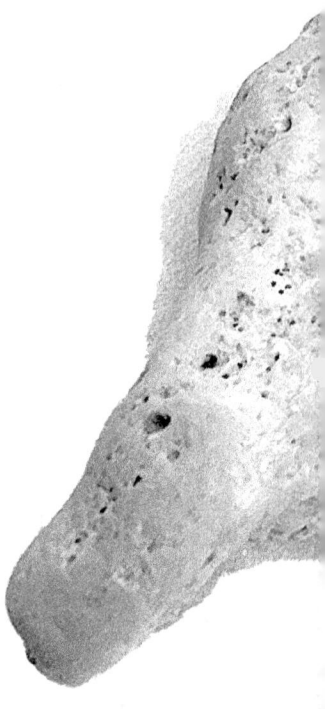

Injured
_hydrus

She is magic
She is the sky
She is a beauty
She simply flies
She is fire
She is fierce
She is the wild
The world she pierced

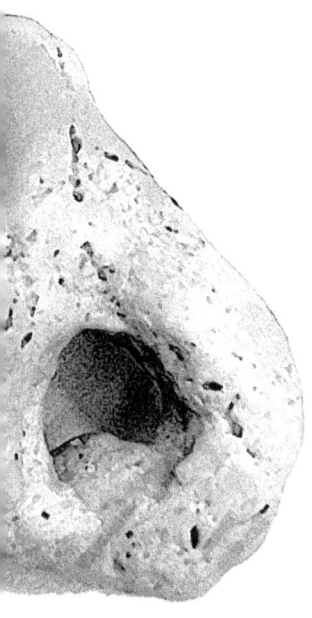

She
_hydrus

The world knows nothing more precious
than each whisper your thoughts make

_hydrus

Thinking about us
I can't even breathe
All thoughts are of you
And they will never leave

Unremitting
_hydrus

You are my every start
An undying finish line
Racing through my heart
With me all the time

Obstacles are many
The ones we will find
Destiny your champion
My champion you are mine

Victoire
_hydrus

You bring out my every shadow
To paint it over with your brush

hydrus

I embraced her spirit
Upon my chest
Our breathless heartbeats
Felt so at rest

Numbing tingles
As we caress
Our morning sunrise
Such a blissful mess

Spoiled
_hydrus

Live life so you can start living

_hydrus

Your words were toxic
The pain was real
I felt all alone
Life a new ordeal

I could not cope
With the pain that came
I lost all hope
In your sick twisted game

But I found a way
To believe in me
Build myself back up
Learn to just be free

I broke the chains
That bound me to you
Now I found myself
And the world is new

Emergent
_hydrus

I hope you heal
Your open wounds
Nature appeals
A witnessed doom

Charity begs
For likes on command
We are always needing
A stranger's hand

Nutured
_hydrus

Sometimes the universe
Sends you a sign
That the heart
Needs to hold
And accept as divine

_hydrus

ENDfinity

A silent voice is stronger
Than a muted scream

_hydrus

You are a spirit
Not from this earth
From the heavens
That gave you birth

You are the mighty
The blazing sun
Full of fire
Burning every one

Fierce your storms
The hearts you jolt
Wings of lightning
Passions your bolt

Grasping the sky
Capturing all space
You are the phoenix
Claiming your place

Boss
_hydrus

She is the morning I never want to end

_hydrus

ENDfinity

Let's kiss
Under the rain
Hold me tight
Forget the pain

In my arms
You need to be
My perfect love
Eternally

No End
_hydrus

Why question
Doubt every choice
Ask about each action
Masking your voice

The inner noises
Keep you awake
They conspire
Play with your fate

Although they pest
Never refrain
Each day a test
Mental the strain

Make them silent
Trust in your soul
You have the will
To snatch control

They are your minions
Pull at their leash
Choke the life
Until they cease

Then live again
Become so free
Delete the questions
Live to be

Unapologetic
_hydrus

You are more than a moment

hydrus

Beneath the branches
Where shadows play
Leaves are whispering
In their gentle way

A celestial tapestry
Under the moonlight
Where the sky meets the earth
And the dreams touch the night

Find your solace
Under the trees
Their roots your anchor
Feel the twilight breeze

Through this rustling
Hear your lullaby
It's your soothing song
Bidding the day goodbye

Adieu
_hydrus

ENDfinity

We are not an illusion
Just reality draped in a magic
Fairytale

_hydrus

I have missed your lips
Tracing down my chest
Sleepless nights
Still cannot rest

Come back to me
Back to your home
Sleep in my arms
Don't be alone

Landfall
_hydrus

Love your beautiful
Because it is all I ever see

_hydrus

Here are the crows
They come again
Blamed for all
But always friends

Scaring the masses
But I love their song
Always with me
When all goes wrong

Watcher
_hydrus

I found a quiet beautiful
Only to moan her name
An earthly stunning angel
No one could ever tame

Her eyes glared in moonlight
With a soul inked by the stars
Each moment that I lived us
Heaven became all ours

Eden
_hydrus

I only look forward because you await me at my end

_hydrus

Sink into my chest
Find a home where you can rest

Let the voices fade away
Close your eyes so I can play

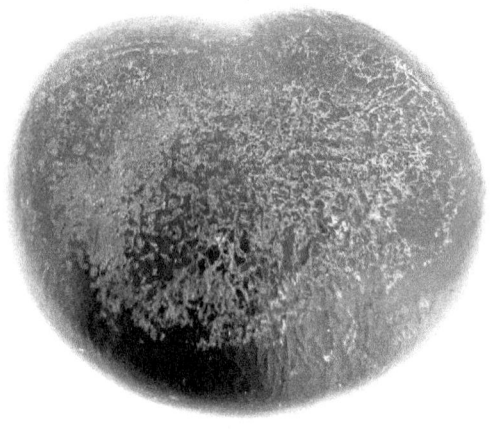

Touch
_hydrus

Your wings protect me
From afar
Give me light
To my dark

Silences chaos
When I weep
An endless love
That never sleeps

Universe
_hydrus

I never knew how to love
Until I fell for her knowing
She would make everything new

We will never meet
But our souls
Have been
In love
For a lifetime

hydrus

I want to quiet the noise
That lives in your eyes
Remove all the tears
That kill you inside

Be the morning after
Wrapped in our feels
Capturing your smile
Reliving what's real

A Moment
_hydrus

In the caverns
Of despair
A silent plea
Was made aware

I found a hero
Weathered my storm
Gave me life
I felt reborn

Our heartbeats echoed
Breaking the chain
A symphony of love
Soothing the pain

In this garden
I found release
Loneliness transformed
Into internal peace

Serene
_hydrus

Life has lost you to the winds...

Liberated
hydrus

but the tides will bring you back

_hydrus

Love is a sunrise
To the soul's expanse
A canvas painted
In the hues of chance

The promise of tomorrow
Hopes melody and song
A start to a new beginning
Or ending a longing wrong

View
_hydrus

In the trials of life
Forge your trail
Let the heart's compass
Guide your sails

Ignore the voices
They irritate
Drowning your song
Just to frustrate

Embrace your path
Let spirits align
A symphony of strength
Where resilience shine

Amidst the packs
Stand tall and true
Enjoy your beauty
And all that's you

Race
_hydrus

You are everything imaginable
An ever compassing wisdom
That only knows the spirit
That is you

_hydrus

  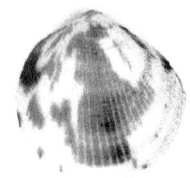 

The farther you are
The closer we feel

_hydrus

The mirror my canvas
Your reflection divine
In every flaw
Unique the design

Ignore the chaos
Of others disdain
For in your gaze
Perfection remains

Peerless
_hydrus

There is no happiness
Unless you make yourself the priority

_hydrus

Any thought
That I make
Fill my dreams
When I'm awake

Life can't ever
Remove your mark
It lives inside me
My endless spark

Match
_hydrus

In life's dark theater
Our hearts entwined
A story written
In the darkest times

Beyond the horizon
Our dreams ascend
Your presence my sonnet
Where love never ends

Signal
_hydrus

In my vivid memory
Your laughter rings
A symphony of joy
The echo clings

Parted by time
By its relentless flow
Faith makes us eternal
In your angels glow

In dreams we meet
Where shadows fade
Together again
Our sweet serenade

Beyond this realm
Where the stars align
I'll find you there
Until the end of time

Woven
_hydrus

You make me forget I'm alive
And make me remember why I live

ENDfinity

Even in darkness
There will shine a light
Calling to your soul
Making the world feel right

Have it lead your heart
Trusting all its might
Surrender your existence
As it becomes your sight

Tranquility
_hydrus

Feel passion for what you do
And greatness will be the product
Of all your sacrifice

_hydrus

In a corked abyss
I lost my way
A drowning anchor
Where I sipped my days

Chains of thirst
Where nostalgia dined
I was a captive soul
In a glass confined

Through that haze
Answers were found
A new path to light
To a sober ground

And if the flask
Would tempt return
I would stay away
Lessons were learned

Siphon
_hydrus

She is as delicate
As a butterflies wings
Her smile flutters
It makes my heart sing

Monarch
_hydrus

ENDfinity

I searched for heaven
And found a life with you

_hydrus

Be kind to all
For you don't know
They carry pain
As we all do

Life is hard
We struggle through
Deal the cards
And just be you

Roulette
_hydrus

You are my endless butterfly
Without a cocoon
Your beauty is so infinite
The sun has found its moon

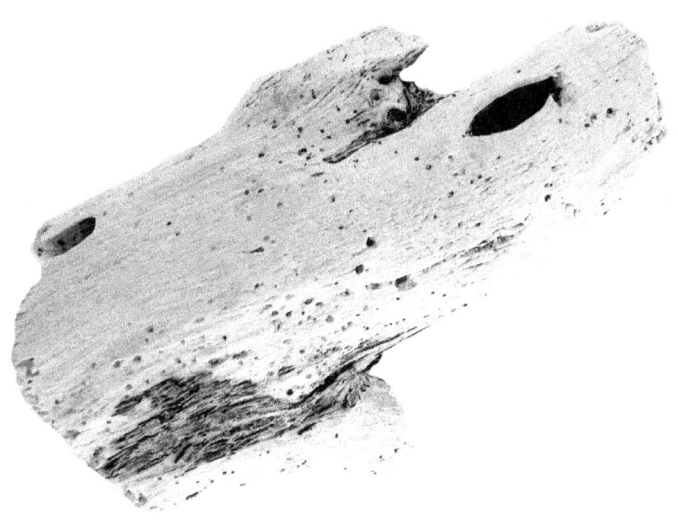

Timeless
_hydrus

Control your today
By eliminating the doubts of tomorrow

_hydrus

Morning whispers
Late night laughs
Slow dances
Endless paths

Long embraces
A simple kiss
Holding hands
I live for this

Meaning
_hydrus

Have faith in the Universe
It was written for you

_hydrus

From toxic shores
I sailed away
A beacon rising
Escaping decay

Cut the chains
That bound my flight
The sun then rose
It renewed my light

The path unwritten
Canvas my own
No longer tethered
Love was overthrown

Self discovery
I reclaim my zest
A new chapter begins
My heart is at rest

Navigate
_hydrus

Hold my hand
Life seems unfair
Countless trials
The world's unclear

I will guide your way
Watch every breath
Believe in us
This is our test

Creed
_hydrus

Your smile reminds me of why I exist

_hydrus

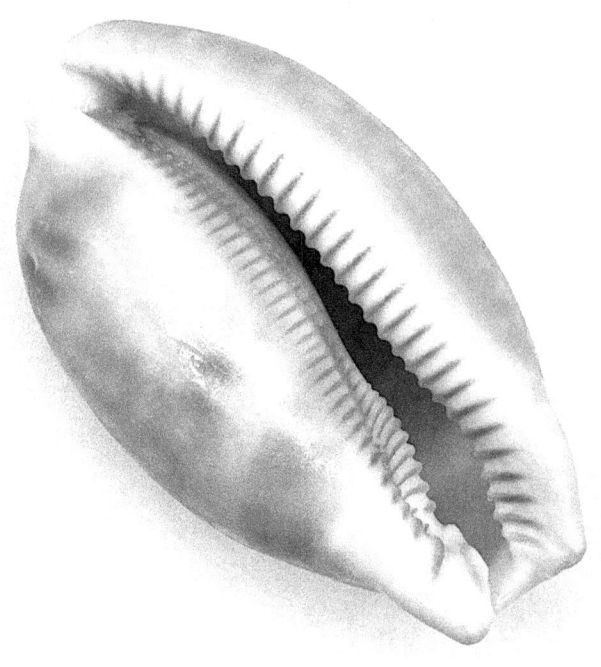

Heaven watches
And she is proud of you

hydrus

ENDfinity

My hands hold the bliss
Of her embrace

Her body bears the prints
And the soul she has traced

Inscribed
_hydrus

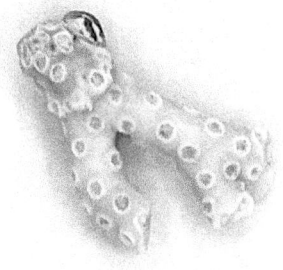

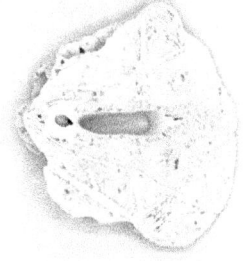

Love can feel your passion
Even if words are never spoken

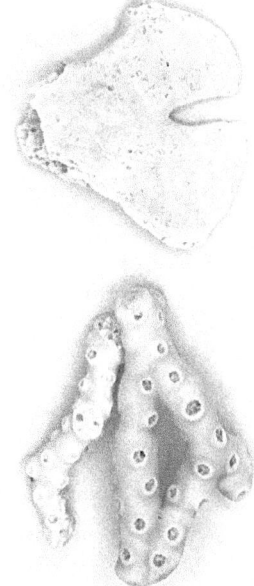

_hydrus

I miss her
When she's not with me
I miss her even more
When she is

_hydrus

ENDfinity

Success will bloom
With every thorn you pluck

_hydrus

Close your eyes
And feel my heart
Grab my hand
And never part

Let's pretend
To fly away
Escape this world
Live out our days

Dreamt
_hydrus

You are the beauty
In beautiful
And I only live
To be full of you

Uncharted
_hydrus

I question myself
And all I do
Was I right
Did I have a clue

I made decisions
They fell apart
Ruined existence
Finished the start

Yet here I am
Feeling alone
No one calls
Silent the phone

Tears they fall
Caress the face
Line my scars
I hide in place

Will I find heaven
Restart the climb
Mend the heart
Regain the time

Strength will find you
Drink from its cup
Taste its power
And get back up

Move
_hydrus

ENDfinity

Give me that smile
That warms up the sun
Showers the clouds
With laughter and fun

I know that it lives
Inside where it sleeps
Not knowing its purpose
Or why it does weep

Surrender your anguish
And open your heart
Let out that sadness
That keeps us apart

I promise to always
Extinguish all tears
Absorb those emotions
Quiet your fears

Amidst
_hydrus

Fall asleep
In my arms
Forget the world
And all its harm

In our nest
We can breathe
Let's be at rest
And never leave

Stay
_hydrus

You made life worth living

_hydrus

You are not alone
We all do bleed
The fight is real
When pain succeeds

A thousand reasons
For all to fail
Just know in life
Love will prevail

Conquer
_hydrus

In the monsters grip
I once did sway
Bound by chains
Of a toxic decay

Through darkness deep
I fought to flee
To break away
From what shouldn't be

With courage born
Of trials endured
I found a path
Where I'm secured

In the gentle hands
Of a day's new light
I discovered peace
In love's pure flight

Indomitable
_hydrus

She was my rose in winter
Sunshine for spring
Laughter should I fall
Summer for all things

Seasons
_hydrus

Live as you dream
Not as you sleep

_hydrus

Lost in time
A love untold
Tale of two hearts
In the times of old

Destiny weaved
A wondrous thread
Reuniting souls
Once thought were dead

Like stars converging
In the southern sky
Love reborn
A celestial cry

In the arms of heaven
Sweet the embrace
A long lost love
Would find its place

Cosmic
_hydrus

She held
My hand
In silence
Until
The noise
Became
Whispers

Sonant
_hydrus

The world might question you
But only your heart will know the truth

_hydrus

Her wings gave me flight
And I lost my fear of falling

_hydrus

ENDfinity

She ran through every thought
Walking in all my dreams
Pulsing to each moaning beat
Living in my every stream

Awakenings
_hydrus

I need to get lost in you
And forget the world even exists

_hydrus

Your quiet smile
Teases me
As you exist
So passionately

Let me caress
Your perfect lips
Our morning bliss
And you I miss

Vigil
_hydrus

Your beautiful darkness redefines the light

I always feel your heaven
When the dusk eats the night
As your waves coat our flesh
And your gardens spring delight

With every passing star
Our heartbeats breathe and sing
Lost in your black skies
Under your dark wings

Paradise
_hydrus

Let's run away
From our everyday
Live on each other's lips
Simply love and play

Lose ourselves forever
New memories to stay
Let's run away together
Never look back on today

Let's
_hydrus

ENDfinity

We were etched in the stars
Before our first day or our tomorrow

_hydrus

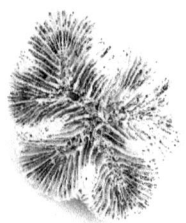

Sail with me
Go back in time
To another world
Where you were mine

We would kiss
To every song
Dancing so tight
Nothing was wrong

Watching the ocean
And the pounding waves
Tides would swell
We would not behave

Letting the world
Witness our fire
And in the sand
We would burn our desire

Habana Again
_hydrus

I questioned my feelings
And all that we did
Replayed countless decisions
And the sins we both hid

But we chose to move on
As the stars wept and cried
Saving us from being us
To live after we both died

Lambs
_hydrus

ENDfinity

Even a second of your bliss
Would last me a lifetime in love

_hydrus

Within your soul
There beats a fight
Unleash the winds
Let doubts take flight

A destined courage
Vibrant it climbs
Vast the landings
Worries behind

Amongst the clouds
You soar and glide
Without the noises
You left inside

The world is endless
It has it all
Your will supports you
To have it all

Destination
_hydrus

You are not broken
Or a piece of a thing
You are a divine perfection
My complete everything

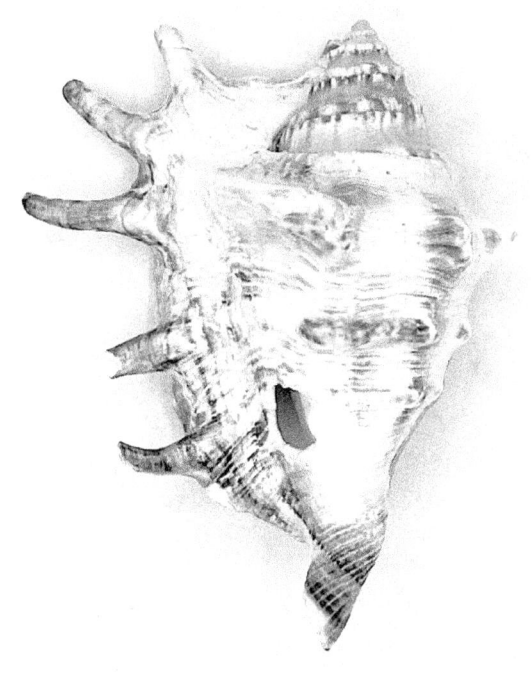

Real
_hydrus

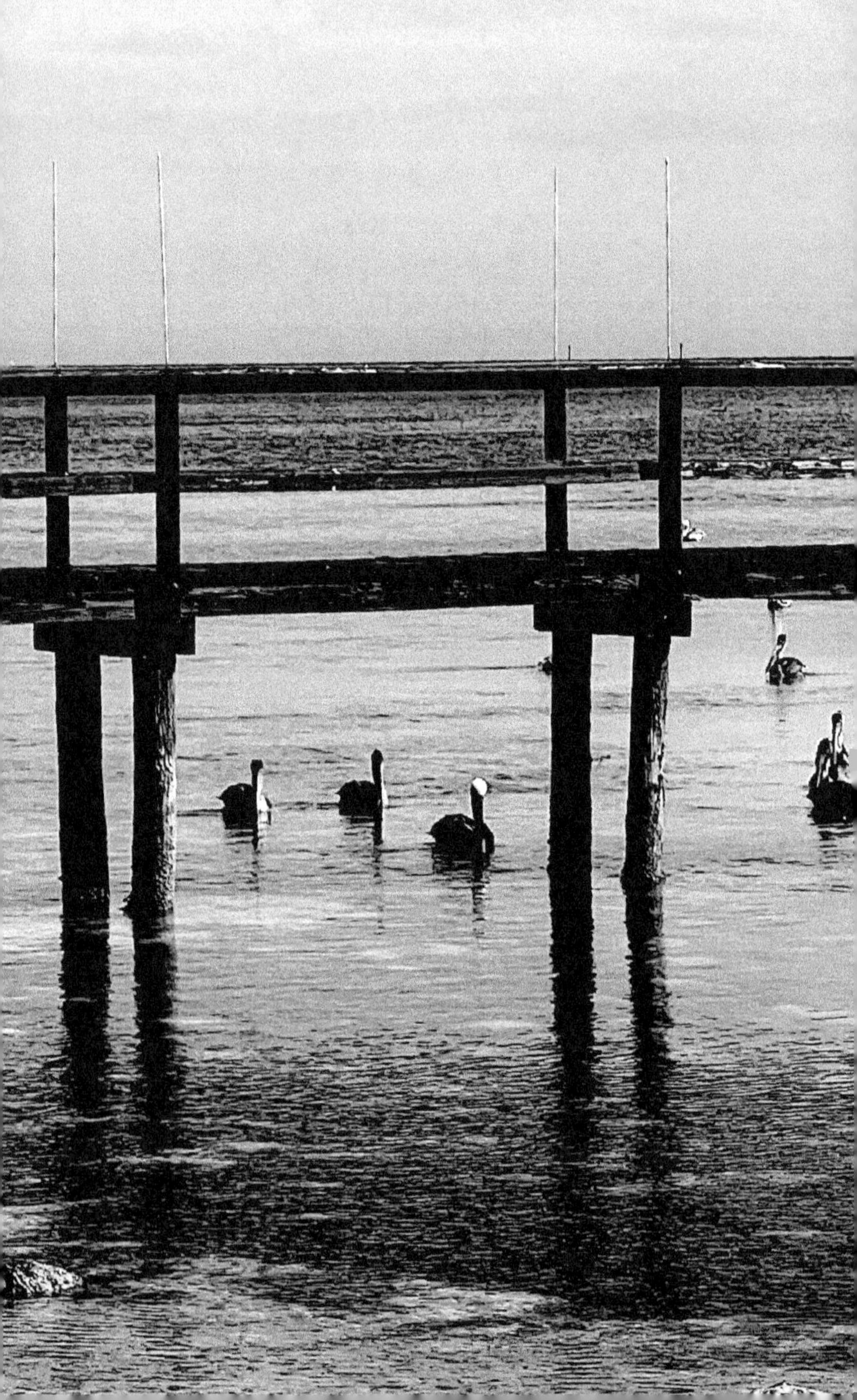

Every bridge will lead you to a new horizon

_hydrus

Words can seem simple
Even when they are read
They become much harder
Once they are said

Be truly mindful
Of how sharp they can feel
They can pierce the heart
Remind you of what's real

Irreversible
_hydrus

In life's odyssey
Dreams brightly unfold
Embracing the storms
Of the new and the old

With passion the compass
Love as our guide
Rise like the sun
And takeover the sky

Interwoven
_hydrus

ENDfinity

Your fearlessness is infinitely beautiful

_hydrus

She hid in the ocean
Behind all of the clouds
Ran into the forest
Where her screams were so loud

Laughing in silence
Her angels appeared
Dressed as the demons
The ones she most feared

Delusions
_hydrus

Your mind will make it happen
Your soul will make it true

_hydrus

She rested her head on my chest
Our bodies laid sweaty and twined
My hands would never find rest
Finding ways to take what's mine

Mine
_hydrus

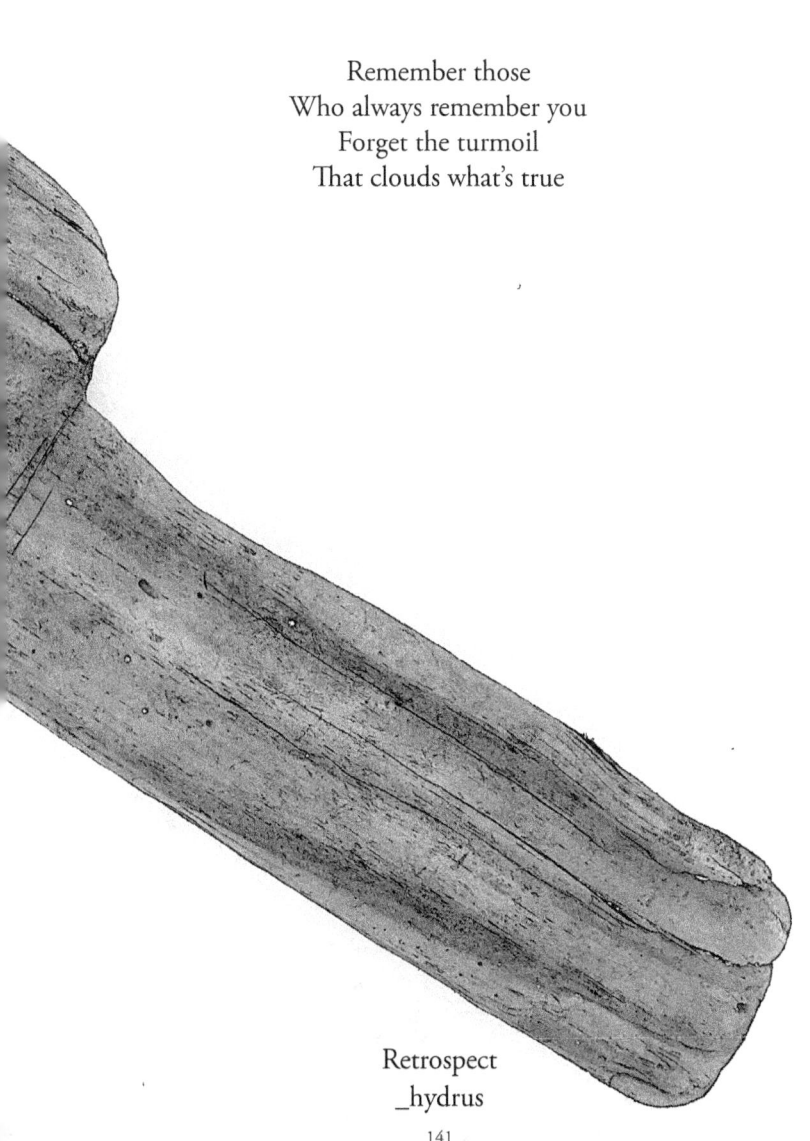

Remember those
Who always remember you
Forget the turmoil
That clouds what's true

Retrospect
_hydrus

Never be the silent voice
To the echoes
That live in your heart

_hydrus

Let me be the one
Who holds you in his arms
Never letting go
Keeping you from harm

Always being close
Being by your side
Living as we love
Knowing what's inside

Threads
_hydrus

I never want to see the sun
If it means leaving you tonight

_hydrus

I wish you saw
What I can see
Heavens beauty
Plus infinity

Pure perfection
Even when you fall
You are my light
My one my all

Glowing
_hydrus

ENDfinity

I found hope in every tear we shared

_hydrus

Focus on your passions
They will propel you to your goals

_hydrus

No one needs to understand your motivation
Or give approval to what your heart commands

_hydrus

ENDfinity

Live by chance
Not by circumstance

_hydrus

Being so far
Wanting you here
Feeling so helpless
Unable to steer

Sending my love
Want you to heal
Remember your worth
And what is not real

Fog
_hydrus

You are so much more
Than what you see

_hydrus

Look outside
Beyond the grass
Reach the horizon
To a sea of glass

Your dreams are waiting
An unbridled view
The winds are swirling
Asking for you

Fly to them
Spreading your wings
Embrace what's yours
Restart the spring

When the sun rises
Washes your eyes
You will be rewarded
With an endless sky

Soared
_hydrus

The days are here
And soon they are gone
Time seems to fly
Yet appears so long

Drowning in thoughts
Of what could be
In the now I live
Of my humanity

Sadness visits
The room goes dark
I search the caverns
That cage my heart

In this moment
I begin to see
I am in control
Of my reality

Prevail
_hydrus

Nothing matters
Unless you matter

_hydrus

There is no such thing as far away
When you carry someone's soul with you

_hydrus

Inside I wonder
If you think of me
Time passes by
You just let me be

My mind always wonders
About you each day
Hoping you return
Hoping you are okay

Thoughts
_hydrus

ENDfinity

Every storm is an opportunity in disguise

_hydrus

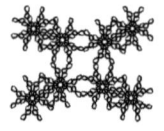

I wake up
To watch the sky
Knowing your soul
Is so close by

Inside my heart
Within this chest
Feeling so loved
Living at rest

Seeing
_hydrus

Searching for you
Through all the rain
The storms enjoy
Replaying my pain

You are the voyage
I need to make
Nothing is greater
All is at stake

Sailing for you
Swimming to shore
Jumping the tide
You I adore

Let our waves
Pound the planks
Claim my heart
Upon the banks

Reach
_hydrus

ENDfinity

Success is sometimes built on failure
Not the lack of it

_hydrus

I discovered humanity
And it blinded my eyes
One could never imagine
The things it defies

Feeding off love
It selflessly acts
Does what is right
Never asks for it back

Gives to the lost
Needing not to be found
Helping the cause
Inspiring those around

If only I could capture
Just a piece of its shine
Life would gain meaning
And all would be fine

Tether
_hydrus

Drifting away
From who I am
Not understanding
There was a plan

A greater place
For me to be
Trust in myself
And I will see

Tapestry
_hydrus

ENDfinity

Even the largest waves meet the sand.
No matter how big it seems, it will pass

_hydrus

We will never be perfect
We will never be fine
We are somewhat broken
But we will mend over time

Glued
_hydrus

176

You are beyond special
The only one of your kind
You conquered all that came
Left everyone behind

Life has been a challenge
Cruel and unrefined
Self love became your mirror
Now truly you're defined

Spiritual
hydrus

Become every chapter
That has never been written

_hydrus

The most beautiful moments in life
are moments when you are expressing your joy,
not when you are seeking it.

Jaggi Vasudev

Love your infinite self
For it endlessly loves you back

_hydrus

Thank You

I just wanted to say thank you to all of you who've been reading and supporting my poetry and my words. Your presence means everything to me and turns all of my writing into something truly special. I cannot thank you enough for all of the love and inspiration you've brought into my world!

Thank you again to my incredible team!
(Cleo & Jojo)
For your consistent dedication, love and devotion. Thanks for your enduring patience in me, (Especially with timelines). You guys are the powerhouse behind Hydrus, and I feel incredibly thankful and fortunate to have you both in my corner.

A huge THANK YOU to my Ravens and the Hydrus Team
(ARC Readers)
for your ongoing love and support. You play such a big part in everything I do, and I'm continually humbled by all you do. You continuosly amaze me with your creativity, passion and kindness. I could never thank you all enough.

ENDFINITY

Playlist

Fix You	ColdPlay
Courage to Change	Sia
Fight Song	Rachel Platten
Unstoppable	Sia
Hall of Fame (feat. will.i.am)	The Script, will.i.am
Don't Give Up	Peter Gabriel
Alive	Sia
Someone You Loved	Lewis Capaldi
Mercury	Sleeping At Last
Princessess Don't Cry	CARYS
Scars To Your Beautiful	Alessia Cara
Beautiful	Bazzi
Lose You To Love Me	Selena Gomez
Girl on Fire	Alicia Keys
Hold on	Chord Overstreet
lovely (with Khalid)	Billie Eilish, Khalid
Keeping Your Head Up	Birdy
Runaway	AURORA
Beautiful Things	Benson Boone
Moral of the Story	Ashe
Sirens	Fleurie
this is me trying	Taylor Swift
Carry You	Ruelle, Fleurie
Runnin' (Lose It All)	Naughty Boy, Beyonce
Rise Up	Andra Day

Listen here:
bit.ly/3VmvUKg

Also by: _hydrus

ENDVISIBLE

A collection of poems about the endless feeling of being invisible while going through the emotions and sometimes cruelties of life. Illustrated by the author's own photography, this book guides us through grief, loss and love in a dark and inspiring way typical to how Hydrus's writing helps us cope with reality.

AWAK**END**

Tarots cards, much like poems, have the ability to paint a vivid picture of what once was or what could be. They delve into the subtleties that we all carry within ourselves and the secrets that make us who we are.

AwakEND is an immersion into the world of tarot and its mysteries. Read it one way, then another, and let the words guide you into the meaning of each card.
Allow chance and curiosity to accompany you on this incredible journey and let your heart awaken to hope even after having thought everything was lost...

And who knows what secrets you might find out about yourself...

DARK**END**

Is a small look into the world I call my reality.
Through poems, photography and art, I try to capture the ups and downs of this voyage we call life, and sometimes I refer to it as just existing.
Embedded in my words are stories of emotions and feelings that range from the darkest of moments to times of having some type of hope for resolve.

Life is raw and ever-evolving, and we always seem to put ourselves last overall. Time proves to be quite relentless. I hope that we all find common ground through our everyday struggles and in the end, understand that love, although painful at times, can provide so many answers.

So the question then becomes "how can we better love ourselves?"

HEART**END**

Is about how we experience love and some of the journeys we embark on when love strikes our heart. It's about the numerous complex phases and ever changing stages of the purest human emotions.
It might be a first kiss, a new romance, a guilty pleasure or a sense of loss but love always helps us reach the heavens or crash down upon its shores.
Love gives even when it takes, it heals and embeds its mark and sculpts us into who we are.

"We all open our hearts and in the end this is the love we bleed."
_hydrus

ENDTHOLOGY

Is a collection of poems drawn up from experiences, thoughts, and emotions. Not everything in the world is dark, but many times we live without any light. We lose ourselves in what we consider our reality. Our souls forget what is important. At the same time, we rejoice when we regain our passion and our inner light.

We might live many lives, but which one will you always remember?

What memories will we ink?

What will have true meaning?

How will we live our END?

_hydrus

ENDLOVE **END**PAIN

A collection of poems that deal with the human struggle of being in love. The emotional roller coaster and the ups and downs that our souls take on this journey. This path is one of endless bliss but some-times agony.

Love is always a conflict of raw emotion and trust. It is a journey we seek to take and at times we regret we do. It is a struggle between good vs. evil but mostly in ourselves.

ENDROAD

An original collection of poetry, comprised of new works, writings, and photography. It documents the many facets of ones inner journey. It deals with our ever-changing emotions, and how the mind and heart react differently when confronted by lifes cruel ironies.

We all live inside and outside ourselves. The quiet whispers we hear and the ones we ignore. The inner voice that makes us passionate, gives us hope, or creates the monster that sharpens their teeth.

ENDroad details the winding aspects of that search for answers. It shows that we all sometimes feel the same. That we are not alone. The paths we take or the ones that take us to mold our humanity into who we are. Each one presents us with the ability for us to rediscover ourselves again.

At times we might feel lost but the truth to finding our way will always rest in our hearts.

My end does not mean I am finished
It only reveals that I am starting again.
_hydrus

WEAK**END**

What happens when life and love clash?
When desire is blinding and passion betrays?
Who do you become and where does it all END?

Welcome to WeakEND, the first book in the FallEND series.

Where we discover a man's journey to answer these questions.

"**Love gave so it could take**" and only his inner demons will keep him from his angels. _hydrus

BROK**END**

Will he ever be able to recover?
Will he be able to find redemption or have a chance at finding true love again?
Or will life just continue to ruin his hopes of finding true happiness.

Sometimes the universe speaks to us in waves, only to watch us drown in its infinite choir of noise. _hydrus

About The Author

Hydrus, is an enigmatic poet shrouded in mystery, who is also a photographer and artist. Within the veiled depths of anonymity, Hydrus pens verses that intricately capture the dance between darkness and the fleeting glimmers of light beyond the shadows. Having authored 10 books, his literary creations have traversed borders, resonating in over 30 countries. His words encompass the vast spectrum of human experience, exploring themes of love, loss, passion, triumph, inspiration, and darkness. Notably, he coined the phrase 'Write your Soul®,' encapsulating the belief that we all can right ourselves through the power of the written word.

Connect with _hydrus:

Website: www.hydruspoetry.com
Instagram: @hydruspoetry
Facebook: www.facebook.com/hydruspoetry
TikTok: @hydrus_ravens
Redbubble Merchandise:
www.redbubble.com/people/hydruspoetry/explore
YouTube:
https://www.youtube.com/@HydrusPoetry